Arduino For Beginners

How to get the most of out of your Arduino, including Arduino basics, Arduino tips and tricks, Arduino projects and more!

Table Of Contents

Introduction

I want to thank you and congratulate you for downloading the book, "Arduino For Beginners".

This book contains helpful information about using your Arduino.

You will learn about the different Arduino types, and the capabilities and restrictions of each. The Arduino is an affordable, yet powerful, computer system that has a large range of uses.

This book will explain to you tips and techniques that will allow you to begin successfully understanding, using, and getting more out of your Arduino! This includes setting it up with different operating systems, writing code, and making cool and fun projects!

The capabilities of your Arduino are virtually limitless. With the help of this guide, you will be well on your way to creating many different and fun projects with the power of your Arduino!

Thanks again for downloading this book, I hope you enjoy it!

CHAPTER 1:
The Basics

The world is increasingly becoming open-source. From the days when we had to rely on the product of proprietary businesses, we can now easily obtain products that can be molded to our specific needs without worrying about license issues and infringements.

However, when the average man thinks of the term "open source", he would most likely think of it as a piece of free software that can be used according to one's wishes. However, the term "open source" is now no longer limited to the intangible -- an Italian company is fast blazing a new trail by making open source hardware.

What is Arduino?

Arduino is basically the newest generation of computing, one that also senses more of the actual, physical world, than our current computers. It is a physical computing platform that is based on the physical board and the development environment used in writing software.

One of the greatest applications of the Arduino is in developing interactive objects, using the various inputs from switches and sensors to control the lights, motors, and the different physical outputs. Projects done on the system can be used either alone, or could be entwined with a software that runs on the computer (MaxMSP, Flash, etc.). The boards can be assembled by hand, or can be used in their preassembled states. The development environment can also be downloaded for free.

Holding its Ground

In fact, Arduino is not the only platform available for physical computing. There are many others, including Phidgets, Parallax Basic, and Handyboard. All of these microcontrollers and microcontroller platforms have one function: make microcontroller programming intuitively easy.

However, Arduino offers distinct advantages not found in the others:

- Cross-platform support. Arduino is known to support not just Windows, but also Linux and the Macintosh OSX. This sets it aside from a lot of competitors that are mostly just available for Microsoft's offering.

- Inexpensive. Unlike how it started (and unlike other competitors), Arduino is relatively inexpensive. This makes the most basic components available for almost everyone. In fact, even pre-assembled modules usually cost no more than $50.

- Simple and clear IDE. The programming environment for Arduino is very easy to use even for beginners, and yet scalable enough for advanced application as well. For the teachers, the system is based on the Processing programming environment -- this makes the students more familiar with Arduino's look and feel.

- Extensible software. As mentioned earlier, Arduino is completely open-source. There are different tools that can be used as extensions by the more experienced programmers. If you know C++, then you can expand the capabilities by using different languages. If you want to understand the intricate details of programming, you can jump from the product's programming language to AVR C, where it is based. Conversely, you can also add the AVR C code into the Arduino programs.

- Extensible hardware. The plans for Arduino's modules are all published under a Creative Commons License. This means that experienced designers can even make their own module versions, refining, improving, and extending it as they see fit. This can also be done by the less experienced among Arduino users -- a breadboard version is available, allowing them to study how it works (and save money in the process).

A Short History

Arduino is an Italian company that started back in 2005. During its first incarnation, Arduino was just a project for students in the Interaction Design Institute Ivrea. At first, the system used a small microcontroller called a "BASIC Stamp", costing about $100 -- an amount that was considered expensive by the students.

The name Arduino comes from a bar in Ivrea, where some of the founders of the project met. The bar itself was named after a King of Italy who reigned from 1002 to 1014.

After the initial concepts, a Colombian student by the name of Hernando Barragan contributed his thesis for a wiring design. This comprised the Wiring platform, from which the researchers worked further on, in order to make the entire item less expensive and more readily available.

Eventually, the school closed. However, the researchers who worked on the project carried on with the idea -- finally evolving it into its latest state.

Arduino's Hardware

In its basic form, an Arduino "board" consists of a microcontroller (Atmel 8-bit AVR) using complementary components that facilitate the board's programming and integration to other circuits. An important part of the Arduino system is the standard connectors, which let users connect the CPU board to different and vastly interchangeable add-ons, which are known as "shields". Some of these shields communicate with the board directly, using various pins. However, there are also shields that can be addressed individually using a serial bus -- this allows shields to be stacked and used in parallel.

Arduino's Software

The Integrated Development Environment (IDE) bundled with Arduino is a cross-platform application that is written in the Java programming language. This heavily derives from the Processing and Wiring IDEs. The software is designed as a way to introduce programming to artists, as well as those unfamiliar with the general rules of software development.

The code editor is a fully-featured one, which has syntax highlighting and brace-matching, as well as automatic indentation. This is also capable of a compile-and-upload command with only a single click. For Arduino users, a program or code developed through this system is called a "sketch".

CHAPTER 2:
Getting Started

What's in the board?

There are several different types of Arduino boards, though only the most basic are described in this book. These boards can be used for a variety of purposes with virtually limitless applications. However, most of these boards have certain parts that are shared among models, performing more or less the same functions.

Power Jack (USB/Barrel). This is the way for every Arduino board to connect itself to a power source. Many kinds of Arduino boards are powered by a USB cable coming out of the wall power supply or the computer.

Aside from serving as a power jack, the USB connection also allows for information to be loaded onto the Arduino for coding. The software will be discussed in detail later.

A note on the power, though: do not use a power supply that is greater than 20 volts, no matter what model you have. This will easily destroy the board. The recommended setting is at around 6-12 volts.

Pins. There are different pins connected to the Arduino board, where you connect the wires needed to construct a full circuit. This is usually used in conjunction with a breadboard, or some wire. There are black plastic headers that will allow you to simply plug the wire into the port. There are different kinds of pins, as well, which are labeled and used for varying functions.

GND (Ground). There are usually several ground pins on the Arduino board, any of which can be utilized to ground and protect the circuit.

5V and 3.3V. These are the power pins. The 5V pin can supply 5 volts of power, and the 3.3V pin can give out 3.3 volts. These measures correspond to the requirements of the simple components used in Arduino.

Analog In. There is an array of pins under the "Analog In" label, running from A0 to different numbers on different models. These pins have the ability to read the signal from any analog sensor, such as temperature sensors. This is also converted into a digital value that can be read by the computer.

Digital. There are also pins on the board that can process digital inputs. Unlike the Analog In ports, however, these can also be used to provide digital output to another component.

PWM. This acronym stands for Pulse-Width Modulation. This is actually part of the digital pin array, marked with tildes (~). These can act both as regular digital pins, and can also simulate a type of analog output (useful for applications such as fading a LED bulb in and out).

AREF. This is the Analog Reference pin, which is quite rarely used. In application, however, this can be used to set an external reference for the voltage. This sets a different upper limit for the analog pins.

Reset Button. There is a reset button that will temporarily connect the reset pin to the ground. This works to restart any code that has already been loaded on the Arduino. If your code does not repeat, this can be a useful feature for testing.

LED Indicator. This is used to indicate the power. This should light up whenever the Arduino board is plugged into any power source. If the LED does not light up, then there might be something wrong with the circuit you created.

TX RX Lights. These are short for "transmit" and "receive" markings. The TX and RX LED lights can give you a handy visual representation of when the Arduino board is sending or receiving any data, such as when receiving a new program from a computer.

Main IC. This is the black rectangle with the metal protrusions that you see. It is the primary integrated circuit, which can be considered as the brain of the Arduino. This component can be different from one board type to another, but Arduino usually utilizes the ATmega ICs created by the ATMEL Company. This is important since you would need to know the IC type along with the board type in order to load up a new program from its software. This is usually easy to obtain, though, as it is found on the top-side writings of the IC. For advanced users, reading the data sheets can reveal the differences between IC types.

Voltage Regulator. This is one of the things in an Arduino board that should not be worked on. It controls the amount of voltage that goes into the board, to avoid overloading. However, it has its own limits -- so as mentioned earlier, your board should not be hooked up to power that is greater than 20 volts.

Meet the Arduino Family

Now that we are familiar with the different components that make up the basic Arduino board, it is also important to know the different kinds of boards and their specific abilities.

Remember that this section only enumerates the basic Arduino boards -- since even the hardware is open source, others can still modify these and produce derivatives with different functionalities and even form factors.

The Arduino Uno (R3)

The Uno will be the ideal choice for someone who is new to the world of Arduino. This board type contains everything you need to get set up. It contains 14 digital inputs and outputs, six of which can be turned into PWM outputs. It also has 6 analog inputs, as well as all the other basics. To power it up, simply connect it to a computer through a USB cable or to an AC/DC adapter/battery.

The LilyPad Arduino

The LilyPad is a wearable, e-textile type of technology. The board type is designed with large pads for connections, and a flat back that allows its integration with clothing using conductive thread. The LilyPad is also washable, with its own family of power, sensor, and input/output components, built especially for e-textiles.

The Arduino Mega

This can be considered as the big brother of the Arduino Uno. It has a total of 54 input and output pins, 14 of which can be used as PWM outputs. It also has 16 analog inputs, and everything else needed for versatility. This type of board is very useful for projects that require a large amount of digital inputs and outputs, such as those that involve lots of LED lights or buttons.

The Arduino Leonardo

This is the first board from Arduino that uses a microcontroller with a built-in USB. This means that the product can be made simpler as well as cheaper. Since the board will be directly handling the USB, certain code libraries allowing the emulation of keyboards, mice, and more, are made available.

The Extended Family

While the Arduino board is integral (and pretty cool) in itself, you can't do much of anything with it alone. The Arduino system is meant to be modular, which means you need to add different items for it to work at its potential.

In this section, you will be introduced to the most basic types of add-ons you can connect your Arduino board to -- sensors and shields. The list we have is far from exhaustive, but you will find here almost everything you need to get a project up and running.

Sensors

As we mentioned before, the Arduino is famous for its concept of interacting with the real world, as opposed to relying on human input. To do this, it interfaces with a very wide variety of sensors that measure the following:

- Temperature

- Light

- Sound

- Degree of flex

- Proximity

- Pressure

- Acceleration

- Radioactivity

- Carbon monoxide

- Humidity

- Pulse

- Barometric pressure

- And a whole lot more!

Shields

There are also Arduino "shields", which we tackled earlier. They are technically just pre-built boards that can be stacked on your main board, giving it additional abilities such as:

- Cellular or wireless communication

- LCD screen control

- Motor control

- Internet connection

- MIDI interface

- And lots more!

CHAPTER 3:
Installing the Software

Now that you have been briefed on the different aspects of the Arduino hardware, it is time to learn more about the other side of the coin: the Arduino IDE. This part of the book will tell you how to install it.

<u>What you need:</u>

- A computer with either a Windows, Mac, or Linux operating system

- Any Arduino-compatible microcontroller (for starters, any of the boards mentioned before would work)

- A USB cable (for the Arduino Uno and some others, this is an A-to-B cable)

For Windows

This guide works for PCs with the Windows XP, Vista, 7, or 8 installed.

1. Download the Arduino IDE through their website. Make sure that you select the version appropriate to your operating system.

2. Unzip your file -- you will see subfolders inside the Arduino folder. Make sure that you do not move any of these folders around while checking, since the file structure is very important.

3. Power up the Arduino by connecting the board to the PC. You should see the power indicator on the board light up.

There is a substantial difference between the installation of the IDE for Windows 8 and Windows XP, Vista, 7. For the latter group, you will have to install additional drivers. For Windows 8, on the other hand, you will need to disable the driver signing feature – the one that protects your computer from the installation of unsigned drivers.

XP, Vista, and 7

1. Plug in the board, and wait for Windows to initiate its driver installation process. This process is bound to fail, but don't worry -- just continue with this guide.

2. Click on the Start Menu, then go to your Control Panel.

3. Go to System Security, then go to System.

4. Open the Device Manager. Look under the Ports (COM & LPT) section. There should be an open port that is named "Arduino <board type> (COMxx). If your Device Manager has no COM & LPT section, you may look under the "Unknown Device" section of "Other devices".

5. Right-click on the identified port and click on the "Update Driver Software" option.

6. Click on the "Browse my computer for Driver software".

7. Navigate to the folder that contains the files you downloaded earlier, then select the Arduino Driver file: "Arduino<board type>.inf". This is located inside the "Drivers" folder, and not the "FTDI USB Drivers" one. If the file is hidden, you may use the "search sub-folders" option.

8. After this, Windows should finish up with the installation.

Windows 8

To temporarily disable driver signing

1. From the Start Screen, open Settings (the Gear icon, which appears when you move the mouse pointer to the bottom-right corner of the screen).

2. Click on the "More PC Settings" option.

3. Click on "General".

4. Scroll down and click the "Restart Now" under the "Advanced startup" menu.

5. After a few moments, click on the "Troubleshoot" option.

6. Click on "Advanced Options".

7. Click the "Windows Startup Settings" menu, then click on "Restart".

8. Once the computer restarts, select the "Disable driver signature enforcement" option from the list.

To permanently disable driver signing

1. Go to the Start Screen.

2. Type in the "cmd" command.

3. Right click on the "Command Prompt", then click "Run as Administrator" on the bottom of the screen.

4. Type or paste the following command:

    bcdedit -set loadoptions DISABLE_INTEGRITY_CHECKS
    bcdedit -set TESTSIGNING ON

5. Reboot your PC, and you're ready to go!

Launching and Testing your Board in Windows

After the installation of the driver, you want to verify that the Arduino board interacts properly with your PC. This is best done by opening a test sketch called "Blink".

1. Launch the Arduino application (make sure the board is plugged in).

2. On the IDE, open File then go to Examples > 1. Basics > Blink.

3. Select the type of the Arduino board you are using by selecting Tools, then going to Board > your board type.

4. Select the COM/Serial port that the board is connected to by clicking Tools, then going to Port > COMxx. If you are not sure which port your Arduino is plugged into, simply remember the ports you currently have then unplug the board. The port that disappeared should contain your Arduino.

5. Once the board is detected and the Blink sketch is ready, press the Upload button.

6. After a moment, the LEDs on your board should flash, and the "Done Uploading" message should appear on the Blink sketch status bar.

7. If everything works as it should, the onboard LED on the board should be blinking -- this is the first program you have uploaded to your Arduino!

For Mac

This part will show you how to install and test the software on a computer running Mac OSX.

1. As in Windows, go to Arduino's download page and download the latest software for the Mac operating system.

2. Unzip the folder and open it to confirm the sub-directories inside. The file structure should be maintained, so make sure that you are not moving any files around while checking.

3. Power up the board by connecting it to your computer, using the appropriate USB cable. You should see the power LED light up as soon as you do so.

4. Move the Arduino app to the Applications folder.

5. Depending on the board type you are using, you might need to install FTDI drivers (this is only for the FTDI chip-enabled Arduino boards). Simply download it from the FDI website, double-click, then follow through with the installer instructions. Restart the computer after installing all drivers.

Testing with the Blink Sketch

To test the connection of your Arduino board to your computer, we will try uploading a sample sketch.

1. Launch the Arduino application on your computer, making sure that the board is plugged in.

2. Go to File, then click on Examples > 1. Basics > Blink.

3. Using the Tools option, select the board type that you have (Board > Board type).

4. Select the serial port where the Arduino is connected, by going to Tools > Port > port code. This usually looks something like /dev/tty.usbserial-xxx or /dev/tty.usbmodemfdxxx. If you are not sure which port your board is connected to, simply note all the ports that appear then unplug the Arduino. The port that disappears is the one linked to your Arduino.

5. With the board connected and detected, press the "Upload" button on the Blink sketch.

6. A moment later, the LEDs on the Arduino should flash, with the "Done Uploading" message in the Blink sketch status bar.

7. Once everything completes successfully, the board's lights should be blinking. This is your first ever Arduino program!

For Linux (Debian, Fedora, Ubuntu)

If you belong to the Linux community, you would know that there are literally hundreds of different "distros" or "flavors" that can be used for the operating system. And of course, installing Arduino on each of these involves slightly different methods. For this part, we will be focusing on three of the most common Linux distributions: Debian, Fedora, and Ubuntu.

Debian

1. First off, the Arduino package needs a dependency if you will be using the Arduino Uno board. You will need to

download at least the librxtx-java version 2.2pre2-3, or higher. This is normally available on the wheezy release, but you can install this from packages.debian.org/librxtx-java.

2. There are two types of packages available to Debian Linux: Arduino and Arduino-core. The first is a full Java IDE, while the second contains only the files needed to make sketches through the command line (this has the benefit of having no Java dependencies). To install either, just type this on the Terminal:

   $ sudo apt-get install arduino

Or

   $ sudo apt-get install arduino-core

For Fedora

1. Make sure that you have installed all of the latest updates by typing the following command into the Terminal:

   $ sudo yum update

2. Next, install Arduino by running the following:

   $ sudo yum install arduino

3. Once you try to run it as a normal user, you might encounter the "Error details: Permission denied" issue. To resolve this, you will need to set the read-write access to the program by running the following command:

   Sudo chmod 777 /run/lock

18

For Ubuntu

1. For Ubuntu 10.10 and newer, Arduino should be available in the Ubuntu Software Center. However, you can also install it using the following command:

   Sudo apt-get update && sudo apt-get install arduino arduino-core

For other Linux distributions, detailed steps (as well as catch-all instructions) are available online, in different sites dedicated to the Arduino technology.

Blink Sketch for Linux

1. After the application is installed properly, do the Blink test by launching the IDE and following the same steps as the Mac OSX counterpart.

CHAPTER 4:
Building Basic Projects

LED Strip Light-Up

Now that you know all the basics of Arduino, it is time to learn about actually programming it and creating projects along the way.

We will start with a fun and simple project dealing with e-textiles -- a simple LilyPad Arduino LED Light-up. To carry this out, you will need a LilyPad Kit that contains the following:

- Rainbow LED strip

- Conducting thread bobbin

- LilyPad coin cell battery holder

- Needles

- Coin cell battery

- Scissors

- Embroidery hoop

- Fabric

- Needle threader

1. Thread your needle using the conductive thread.

2. Using an embroidery hoop, set your fabric until it is taut.

3. Make a "positive trace" -- a mark on the fabric that leads from the power supply to the LED strip's positive side.

This trace will start from the battery pack. Place the battery pack (without the battery) near where the LED will be put, making sure that one hole with the plus sign and another with the negative sign is pointed towards the LED's location. These holes are the positive and negative pins of the battery pack. Once the battery pack is in place, you can start sewing. Trap the edge of the board in the fabric by wrapping the thread three times on each positive pin on the board (there is a second one on top).

1. When you sew these pins, do not do it in one big stitch. This tends to be loose and will often move around, touching other components and causing short circuits. It is best to sew using a running stitch.

2. Continue the stitch using the same thread to the positive side of the LED strip, sewing it down like the two other positive pins. Double-check to make sure that you got the correct pole, as the LED won't light up if the opposite pole is connected.

3. Next, you will be doing the negative trace. This will return from the current LED strip to the negative side of the pack. Follow the same instructions as earlier, but this time going the other direction.

4. Make sure that the thread does not have any dangling parts, and that the positive and negative traces do not touch in any part.

5. Put the battery into the pack -- your LED should light up immediately! Congratulations on creating your very first basic Arduino circuit! And on an e-textile, too!

Heating Blanket

If you think that the first project was too easy, that's because it is -- it does not yet involve any programming; it's just about telling you how to create a simple circuit. For this project, we will step up the ante by creating something useful -- a heating pad warmer blanket!

Here are the things you will need:

- 2 5x15 Heating Pads

- N-Channel MOSFET 60V 30A

- Wall Adapter Power Supply (5V DC 1A)

- LilyPad Arduino board

- Red hook-up wire

- Black hook-up wire

- Blue LilyPad LED light

- LilyPad button board

- Conductive thread

- Switch

We won't go into the part of sewing your hand warmer blankets -- we will leave that to your creativity! Instead, we will focus on the circuit.

1. Following the sewing pattern we did during the first project, use the conducting thread to sew the LilyPad board and connect its edges to the positive side of the blue LED lights. The negative parts are all sewn together to connect with each other.

2. Using the red hook-up wire, connect the positive contact of the Arduino board to the positive side of the switch. Use a parallel connection to connect it simultaneously to the positive contact of the heating pad. Make sure to solder this connection instead of using conductive thread.

3. Connecting the negative part is a bit more complicated. Use the black hook-up wire to connect the negative part of the board to the negative contact of the power source. This is then connected to the negative contact of the switch.

4. Create a parallel connection to the "S" leg of the MOSFET.

5. Create another parallel connection to a 10k resistor.

6. Hook up the 11th pin on the LilyPad to the "G" leg of the MOSFET, with a parallel branch to the other end of the resistor.

7. Connect the "D" leg of the MOSFET to the negative contacts of the heating blanket.

8. In the Arduino IDE, use the following code:

language:C

```c
/*
Hardware Connections:
-led1 = D9;
-led2 = D10;
-led3 = D11;
-button = D2;
-Mofset = D3;
*/
int btnPin = 2;
boolean btnPressed = false;
int fetPin = 3;
int led1 = 9;
int led2 = 10;
int led3 = 11;
int mode;
void setup() {
  // initialize the digital pin as an output.
  pinMode(btnPin, INPUT);
  pinMode(fetPin, OUTPUT);
```

```
  pinMode(led1, OUTPUT);

  pinMode(led2, OUTPUT);

  pinMode(led3, OUTPUT);

}
// the loop routine runs over and over again forever:
void loop() {

  //Increment mode on depress, unless mode = 3, then reset to 0

  if (btnPressed && digitalRead(btnPin) == LOW)

    mode = mode == 3 ? 0 : mode + 1;

  //Assign button state

  btnPressed = digitalRead(btnPin);

  switch (mode)

  {

    case 0:

      analogWrite(fetPin, 0); //off

      digitalWrite(led1, LOW);

      digitalWrite(led2, LOW);

      digitalWrite(led3, LOW);

      break;
```

```
        case 1:

            analogWrite(fetPin, 85); //33% duty cycle

            digitalWrite(led1, HIGH);

            digitalWrite(led2, LOW);

            digitalWrite(led3, LOW);

            break;

        case 2:

            analogWrite(fetPin, 170); //66% duty cycle

            digitalWrite(led1, HIGH);

            digitalWrite(led2, HIGH);

            digitalWrite(led3, LOW);

            break;

        case 3:

            analogWrite(fetPin, 255); //100% duty cycle

            digitalWrite(led1, HIGH);

            digitalWrite(led2, HIGH);

            digitalWrite(led3, HIGH);

            break;

    }

}
```

This code allows you to hit the switch to turn on the heating pads; hitting the button to adjust the warmth of the heating elements is also possible. The LED lights will indicate the heat level.

Remember that these two projects are just illustrations -- with these fundamentals as a base, you can use the skills learned to create variations and ultimately, come up with more advanced projects!

CHAPTER 5:
Tips and Tricks

With the previous chapter, we have learned to make beginner-level Arduino projects. As mentioned before, there are virtually countless projects that can be made and you are bound to make a lot of discoveries along the way, too.

This chapter showcases some of the nifty tips and tricks you should know to make building Arduino projects easier and more fun!

First off, be careful when buying an Arduino board. There are lots of official boards and mods that you can use, though they each have their own quirks. For example, some boards are made to be embedded, without any programming interface -- this needs to be bought separately. There are those that can be run from a 3.7V battery, while others need a minimum of 5V to power-up.

Though we have only discussed the basics in this book, you will in time progress to advanced programming such as Processing and Logic.

For Logic, remember that the Arduino module can pick up two different kinds of signals -- digital and analog. Digital is the type of signal that can be made by a button or a trigger. In the Arduino IDE coding language, "on" is registered as "high" and "off" is read as a "low". On the other hand, analog signals work much like dimmer knobs, where the signals are not simply on and off. This separates the value numerically from 0 to 1023.

For Processing, it can get a bit more complicated. As you work your way through, you have to mind a few more specs -- for example, you have to make sure that the components' baud rates match. Also, it is extremely important that you are reading off the right port. If you will be sending out a variety of sensor values, it will be worthwhile to remember as well how many bytes are expected to be sent. This allows you to know how to properly parse out the data (you will learn about this with practice).

Arduino can be considered as the next frontier in the quest for technological advancement. For the first time, machines that can interface with the world directly are in the hands of hobbyists and regular -- even beginners and children -- programmers. This book is just a jumpstart to conquering this frontier -- who knows what cool and immensely useful projects you can make with this great tool?

Conclusion

Thank you again for downloading this book!

I hope this book was able to help you learn more about how to use your Arduino!

The next step is to put this information to use, and begin getting more out of your Arduino!

Finally, if you enjoyed this book, please take the time to share your thoughts and post a review on Amazon. It'd be greatly appreciated!

Thank you and good luck!